UNTANGLED

ALLEGORIES OF THE MIND

Untangled- Allegories of the Mind
Edited & Compiled by Dhanvi Nirmal
Print Edition

First Published in India in 2021
Inkfeathers Publishing
New Delhi 110095

ISBN 978-93-90882-10-6

www.inkfeathers.com

UNTANGLED

ALLEGORIES OF THE MIND

Edited & Compiled by

Dhanvi Nirmal

Inkfeathers Publishing

DISCLAIMER

The anthology "Untangled" is a collection of 7 Stories and 42 Poems by 32 authors who belong to different parts of the globe. The anthology editor and the publisher have edited the content provided by the co-authors to enhance the experience for readers and make it free of plagiarism as much as possible. Unless otherwise indicated, all the names, characters, objects, businesses, places, events, incidents- whether physical/non-physical, real/unreal, tangible/ intangible in whatsoever description used in this book are either the product of the author's imagination or used in a fictitious manner. Any resemblance to actual persons, objects, entities, living or dead, or actual events is purely coincidental. The stories & poems published in this book are solely owned by their respective authors and are no way intended to hurt anyone's religious, political, spiritual, brand, personal or fanatic beliefs and/or faith, whatsoever.

In case, any sort of plagiarism is detected in the stories and/or poems within this anthology or in case of any complaints or grievances or objections, neither the anthology editor, nor the publisher are to be held responsible for any such claims. The author(s) who holds the rights to the story(s) and/or poem(s), shall be held responsible, whatsoever.

CO-AUTHORED BY

Laure Lacornette | A Low Kick | Maria Wynnckyj

Archana Natarajan | Valerie Hernandez

Dhwanie Shetty | Mara Martins | Nehal Gandhi

Yohan Acosta | Aishwarya Shukla | Athena Thiyam

Ishwari Salunke | Malay Mundra | Rebecca Hilliard

Keegan Cockin | Vidhi Jain | Despina Sarakatsani

Grace Heart | Amala Susan Roy | Anushka Kharbanda

Sellina Mutiara | Suchitra Satapathy | Rida Hassan

Samantha Marsters | Nitya Aggarwal

Eider Muñiz Mercadal | Sudipti Saha | Adela Lily

Brianna Kidd | Adlina Khusairi | Nehali Naik | Preethi

CONTENTS

Dhanvi Nirmal
Editor & Compiler

Dhanvi Nirmal is just another sixteen-year-old trying to make a change in this world. She prefers to be called enigma as her pen name and she believes that words have the power to change the world, and so she writes. She writes to survive, make the world a better place and the proof is her page @enigmaspoetry.

This book is a devotion to all the mental health survivors. I see you, I believe in you. The sole purpose of this book for me is to let all the people out there suffering know that they aren't alone. I believe steps like this will help in fighting against the stigma around mental health and so I decided to compile an anthology based on mental health. I'd like to thank Inkfeathers, all the co-authors and my family, friends for providing the utmost support.

Dhanvi Nirmal

Editor

STORIES

1

A LOST LONE WOLF

by Laure Lacornette

There is a plane flying above me. My eyes are closed, I can hear it. The afternoon is already there and I am still asleep. It's getting hard to get up these days. All I want to do is sleep, rest and spare my mind from thinking too much. Because as soon as I am awake that's what I do: I overthink.

"I have no job for the moment. Should I try to go back to the one I had? It was paying more but it was so tiring and bringing me less. There's this one I applied for, they told me it was ok and that they would call back but it is taking time.

Two weeks now. And, finally, do I really want to have a job? To be working only to be able to put something in my stomach. I would want to do something that I like, but what do I like?

Oh, and if I don't find a job, how will I pay my rent? *Those bills.*

I already don't eat as much as I should be doing everyday... I'm stuck here while I would like to get away, but, where to go?"

And it continues – a layering of thoughts, questions, and doubts. It tortures me. It's all duty and obligations. No time to find a way where I could enjoy a few things at times. I am not complaining nor judging, only acknowledging.

In the middle of the day, I am hungry and angry and doubtful about almost everything. I know that I should feel blessed for what I have already, and I do, I really do. Deep inside, I know that I am a fair person with pure intentions; as true as I can be.

So, why do I feel like the worst? A lost lone wolf.

That's what our existences are: contradictions. Everything is not all black or all white. It is black and white and full of different colours at the same time. Things appear blurry while, in fact, it's all clear.

Living is basically easy, existing is not. To exist is to have a will to live; it is to give a meaning to life. Originally, life has none, but you need to find a meaning to it. That is what will keep you from falling, as an invisible protection, in the limbo of despair. The rougher the path, the truer and deeper the meaning, I guess.

This meaning, we have to find it within ourselves, by ourselves and for ourselves. Once found, will it make things easier right away? No, for sure it won't. It will only make things more bearable, day after day, and, perhaps, with some time, you will feel that it is easy.

Of course, words like: "The sun will rise once again, and everything will be beautiful..." find resonance within ourselves, they make us feel a little bit better for some time and it is absolutely fine. But, it is already beautiful, even in this mess. Right where you are, in this precious moment, it is easy, it is beautiful, and it is fine.

The day is going by.

From the middle of the day to the middle of the afternoon. I wake, slowly, and I close my eyes. My mind is calm. It feels as if I had written down my thoughts while asleep.

I listen.

There is another plane flying above me. Fresh air is coming from the half-opened window. I am doing my best. No whistling birds. Only the sound of pigeon's wings nearby.

The city... I remember. I forget.

The evening is rushing.

Soon the sun won't be up no more.

Is it the moment to get up?

Isn't it the perfect moment to get up and go by?

2

ANOTHER DAY (IN THE CITY)

by Laure Lacornette

A shadow, a car and a million impossibilities lying in the dark. A star could stir the sum of all that I let go of. At this time, at this moment, I am no longer shifting, lifting or trying. In this state, there is either too much or not enough time. The sun is shining and right after, the hail is pouring. Leaves are turning red and this window is not big enough to see all of the clouds in the sky.

I am crying with no tears, rather, words are my tears. Letters giving a face to sadness. I am at the brim. The cup is full of sorrow. There is no hope anymore, no dream, no excitement, and no good surprise. I don't feel the weight anymore. It is too heavy on me and I keep going deeper. I dig inward and I learn more about myself. Knowing me and being true to it is all I can do; it is the least I can do.

Tomorrow I might feel different, I surely will…

A year – that is what it takes for the Earth to revolve around the sun. 365 days is what it took for me to attain a sense of realization: I don't change, I evolve, I continue, I go on but I don't change - here. What do I want, where to go? I have no idea. I am miserable but I almost feel free. I thought time would tell, but it's only killing me.

My throat is burning. My head is aching. Dizzy, I will be the last one still waiting. And I am still writing these lines, without a meaning, without a purpose. Is it really helping?

This is my realm. A sad box. Grey heavy skies. Uncertainty, questions with no answers, reveries, duties, evaporated passions. Beneath that, there is truth, a loyal and kind heart, wonders in the most simple moments, admiration, and bravery. Years are shedding apart layers of unnecessary purposes, dead dreams, failures. In an instant, it could all stop and nothing would be left.

It is hard to stay centered when there is basically no center. When you know that there is no meaning to this masquerade but to the one you are willing to create for yourself. That alone will give you the strength to get up in the morning and keep going through your days.

My sanity lies in nature, the oceans, and the waves crashing over the rocks. It runs on the trunks of trees, jumping from branches to branches. It blows in the wind, delicately falls with the snow, dries under the warm rays of the sun and sleeps tight and sound under the moon. No matter how harsh she can be, nature is way better and sweeter than the 'modern' society we live in. The light is getting dark. Life is fading away a little faster every day. A key is turning in the lock. A window is closing and we are all losing.

I am still trying to pour my heart out here, by any means. There is no other way to accept what needs to be taken from the deepest parts of us. The remedy does not exist. With little luck, we will find a place to quit, some doors to close and others to open. Someday, you will see a twinkling star. You will get closer to it and realize that it is a beacon beam. You will notice that it is an ocean you are drifting in, but also, that there is a shore in sight. A vivid ocean is what life is. You don't ask for anything, but you are immersed in it. Trying to cope the best possible way, with whatever comes or doesn't for the rest of your time. Still there is magic to be found, and that is what I will look for as soon as my eyes open.

A shadow. A car. Night fell.

Another day in the city.

3

BRAINDEAD

by A Low Kick

Waking up two hours before what was required to get to my office on time in the evening and exercising mildly has been my routine. I had to do this regular habit since I opted for the night shift in the call center five years ago. It was nothing new to me when the police found me blowing off steam down across the park. It had come as a shock to me when I was taken to the station for questioning regarding the murder of my co-worker and best friend, Aakrit. It had left me aghast in fact. Aakrit, Kalpan and I had been the best team in the hive-A7 of the customer care department hired by TechSols Pvt. Ltd.

The crime scene was even more horrifying. The murderer had used a blunt knife and slit his neck open. The blunt knife which had been used, for as long as I knew, was to open up coconuts to safeguard its owner's fingers and in the process had ended up killing him with a lot of pain. His face held an expression of surprise and strain. Aakrit's mouth was found gagged with his socks and his limbs were tied to the four posts of the bed.

I still remember how the questioning at the police station had gone.

***

"Did he have any enemies?' the police inspector had asked."

"Aakrit did not have any enemies or any financial problems as far as I know sir. We used to work in night shifts and thus we never had any opportunities to even interact with anyone else other than the ATM machines along the roads."

"Any financial problems? Illegal dealings?"

"Nothing that I know of sir, and it is highly unlikely".

"What about his relationship with Kalpan, your other friend? Anything peculiar?"

"No sir, we were good friends. He was a kind of guy who would apologize to a fly for moving around while it would be sucking his blood."

"Hmm. Fine, you may leave for now. Don't think about leaving the city and report in the station immediately when asked to."

"Sir, just one more thing"

"Yes, what is it?"

"Could I have my Swiss knife back?"

"Why? What do you do with it?"

"I use it for opening juice bottle seals, cutting apples etc. during work."

"Yeah sure, take it as you leave."

"Thank you, Sir".

***

It had been very quiet in the office the following week. No one spoke to us about it, but Kalpan and I were often stared at across the entire place.

The following three months were entirely uneventful and empty like the stares we were subjected to, and gradually things had settled back down, Aakrit had been replaced by a new employee, Moorthy, while Kalpan and I had now become the new duo of the hive-A7.

It was after these three months when one day at 4 pm I received a call from Kalpan that woke me up from my slumber. It had been a long night and there was this specific customer who had got on my nerves for two long whole hours mercilessly.

"What is it, Kalpan? Why are you calling me at this hour there is still more than 3 hours to the office."

"What the hell are you saying Srijan? It's time to go to the office and everyone is late."

"Shut up let me sleep, you idiot, you know I have had a headache since last night."

I know that I wasn't exactly polite either but you don't expect a man to reply kindly after you do something like this. I had expected that Kalpan would explain what he was trying to achieve with that weird conversation over the phone, but there was no talk about it the whole night.

After a couple of more uneventful nights and days, I received a call from Kalpan at noon waking me up from my sleep - irritated. He was asking me if I wanted to go for a jog with him.

Wouldn't you be frustrated if you and your friend are working a night shift where you reach home at 9 in the morning and you get a call at 12 in the afternoon for a jog? I mean, seriously, this dude told me at work last night that he won't wake up till 5 in the evening! Such a person is either a prankster with a shitty taste for pranks or doesn't belong to the earth I live on. He's done this a couple of times before and II don't know why I never confronted him in the office about it. The number of calls from Kalpan increased in my call log everyday. Every now and then he asked me out for something silly like a movie, or shopping or for an afternoon jog. Sometimes, his plan ideas were even more serious and hilarious like a tour or hiking. Each time he called I used to let him have it. I called him all sorts of names, insulted him in every verbal way I knew, and yet he didn't stop. 4 more months had passed since then and he still called me every other morning.

One evening while I was jogging down the pavement from the park, I caught a glimpse of Kalpan loitering around my duplex. However, on close observation, I couldn't find him. Thinking of him to be a product of my imagination caused by my irritating thoughts, I didn't think much upon it. That night again was uneventful. I managed to meet my deadlines, finish extra work, shouted a bit at Moorthy for his inefficiency, and kind of apologized later over a cup of coffee with me later on. I was done by 7 AM. I finished another cup of coffee with Kalpan before driving back home.

It was like any other usual day at work but I don't know why I was overly exhausted and sleepy. It was like the body itself was asking me to shut down and slip into slumber. When I woke up it was already three in the afternoon. I had been sleeping with all my limbs spread out and the exhaustion had left my body completely.

With my back still aching a bit I tried to get up.

Suddenly, it hit me.

I hadn't been sleeping with all my limbs outspread! They were actually tied to my bedposts. I struggled to break the ropes but it was all in vain. Trying to find out the moron was who had put me in this position, I started to strain my neck to look in all directions. Kalpan was sitting on my armchair brandishing my Swiss knife in his hands.

"What the heck you moron, untie me right now!"

Kalpan was acting as if he couldn't hear me. I called out louder this time again, but even that was to no avail. It was then when I started to panic and cried for help.

"Help, Help! Someone help! This man has gone crazy. Please, Help!"

Kalpan got up from my armchair and walked upright above my head. Before I could say anything else he had already slit my throat. I gasped for air, once, twice thrice, but it was of no use. I knew I was about to die.

It was extremely painful and completely beyond my understanding.

With a couple of gasps and aghast looks towards Kalpan, suddenly the pain stopped and everything vanished. I was in a state of bliss.

***

The next time I regained my consciousness it was in a police station. Surprisingly, no one was able to hear me, see me or even know that I was there. After a few minutes I saw Aakrit lurking around the corner, and it was after seeing him that it hit me.

I was dead and I guess ghosts do exist.

He saw me and winked, I went ahead to see what he was looking at, it was a man who was being interrogated by the inspector.

"Your name?"

"Moorthy."

"Did you know the deceased?"

"Yes sir, he has been my senior at work since I joined hive-A7."

"Were you close?"

"I would say so sir. He was quite friendly with me in general."

'Would you know if he had any enemies?' the police inspector had asked.

'Sri did not have any enemies or any financial problems as far as I know. We work in night shifts and thus we don't have any opportunities to even interact with anyone else other than the ATM machines along the roads.'

'Any financial problems? Illegal dealings?'

'Nothing that I know of sir, and it is highly unlikely.'

'What about his relationship with Kalpan, your other friend? Anything peculiar?'

'No sir we were good friends and Kalpan is the kind of guy who would apologize to a fly for moving around while it would be sucking his blood.'

'Fine, you may leave for now, and don't think about leaving the city and report in the station immediately when asked to.'

"Sure sir, just one more thing..."

"Yes, what is it?"

"Could I please have my screwdriver back?"

Aakrit started to laugh, even I could not hold my smile back.

***

Approximately 3.5 million people in the United States and 7 million worldwide are diagnosed with schizophrenia and it is one of the leading causes of disability. It occurs due to a lot of overwork and sleeping disorders. It puts a person in a constant state of emergency. The person diagnosed with schizophrenia is always under the impression that other people are trying to monitor him or kill him, and they express very strong emotions towards them. Severe cases may even lead to crime. Thus contact a therapist if you have a doubt about yourself or your near ones. And always follow the rule of *'Early to Bed'*.

4

PHANTOM

by A Low Kick

Tushar's Narration

I won't linger around to tell you all the books I have read, who my ancestors were or any other unnecessary things. It has always been my motto to get straight to the point; it helps in my line of business. When I was young, I met with an accident. Our car had crashed into a trailer, and things got pretty ugly for us.

I survived but my driver succumbed to his injuries. The bones of my left arm were completely crushed and my head was strongly hit. My hand had to be amputated. It was horrible.

After losing all friends and contacts and facing a lot of discrimination from all kids in all the schools I ever enrolled in, my father finally decided to home school me. Deep down, I was glad he made that decision.

Initially, I felt nothing in my left arm. It had turned numb. However, after a week I started to feel it, as if it had grown out again out of nowhere. The only regrettable part was that this new hand was hideous. It had a very thick skin, comparable to animal hide, with scales on it. My fingers were big, bruised, with long nails. And this new left hand of mine constantly itched, and I couldn't scratch it no matter how much I tried. There was no such feeling in my right arm and it remained normal. When I complained about my new left arm being hideous and constantly itchy, the first reaction that I received from my parents and mentor was of confusion, and bewilderment. It was as if they couldn't see it. In a house filled with people, my parents and all the staff, I for the first time in my life, felt alone, as if no one could understand me.

Having a hideous-invisible-to-others left arm wouldn't have been much of a problem if that would have been the end of it. But that was not all. Since the accident I had started to see some unbelievable beings that no one had ever seen before - in front of my eyes.

For example, one of the things I saw was a figure that had claws for hands, hooves for legs, and a cow's head resting on his neck. Another one had a hand that had a hammer attached to it instead of fingers and a beak instead of his mouth. Some had extremely big sized bodies, while others were too small to believe. When I kept complaining about these beings being a constant bother, others told me that I am hallucinating and no such beings existed. It wasn't long until everyone in the house began treating me like a mad guy.

There were times I was afraid to speak about things to avoid questioning gazes and looks of pity across the place. These complex emotions of pity, curiosity, and sympathy had started to irritate me a lot because all of them lacked understandability. I had no idea why this kept on happening to me.

I wanted it to stop.

I was ready to give away everything in my life in exchange for these absurd things to stop and such horrifying beings to stop looking right into my eyes. In addition to my irritation from my treatment in the house, the constant itchiness in my left arm had become quite normal. I often had angry outbursts, which ended up adding to my insanity reports in the house.

Because of this, my entire childhood went to take a dump. My years of adolescence that followed, gave me a golden opportunity that came as a divine light among the darkness of a life I had spent until now.

I got selected in the college of Mass Media Communication with a scholarship when they read my articles on the subject of 'loneliness'. No boasting over there from my side, but they said that the articles were quite exceptional and fantastic. I knew by now that there was no way possible to get rid of the weird beings that followed me my entire life, but now, I could get rid of all that unnecessary sympathy and pity love. It was then, exactly ten days before my departure, when my father received a note from the very same doctor, who had dragged me out of the frying pan of death into the fire of life. It said that he wanted to meet me and everyone in the house and finally explain 'something' as he said it in the note.

Dr. Saral Sugam's Narration

It was thirteen years ago when a small child of three was brought into the emergency ward of the hospital. All bones in the left upper limb crushed, he would have to do without it from now on, and a hit on the head; possibility of an internal injury. Evidently, he had been in an accident. As the presiding surgeon in the hospital, I took up the case. The boy survived with a limb gone and a blind spot created due to some damage in the optical lobe of the brain, and even though the injuries were quite healthy within a week for discharge. I kept on seeing him until his wounds healed.

I kept on seeing the boy until he was five, his wounds had healed, he needed not come in my office again and was good to go. It seemed that he wanted to say something but his father evaded the entire thing.

Only last evening, I received a letter from the father of that child, stating the entire case of complications that he referred to as insanity of his child. He asked my opinion if it was safe for his child and others if he sent him to college where he apparently had earned a scholarship. I knew that it would have been unwise if I explained all the complications in a letter, just so that I could avoid travelling. Such talks are meant for a proper face to face conversation only. I sent them a note that I would like to see the boy personally and would like to tell everyone something.

After six hours of travelling, I reached the house, and I saw a chauffeur waiting for me to accompany me into the place. He directed me to the verandah, where I was welcomed by the entire family and their staff. Among the gentle introductions and murmur, I saw the boy. He was wearing a scorn on his face and scowled admirably when our eyes met. Others seemed to be unaffected by such handsomely rude behaviour. I walked up to him and raised my left hand. He looked at me gaping, before he could reply, I scratched his left cheek.

"Do you feel relieved?"

The boy was utterly amazed and startled.

"How? How in the world did you do it? It was my arm and I wasn't able to do it since the past 13 years... Can you see it? Can you see my left arm? Can you see how hideous it looks?" He asked.

"It's not hideous as it looks to me, young man. It's just a matter of perspective."

Well without a doubt, this stunt had left the entire household astounded beyond capacity. It took a few minutes for everyone to come back to their senses.

"If you could all sit down, I can explain." I said.

Everyone found a seat immediately and were eager to listen.

"Let's start with why Tushar sees and feels his lost left arm? This is nothing strange; many patients who lose their limbs experience the same thing. It is called the Phantom Limb Phenomenon, studied majorly by a renowned doctor during the African war. So many injured soldiers returned home with a phantom limb.

How can Tushar feel a left hand that no longer exists? That's because the brain transmits a sensation. Now then why would the brain transmit the wrong sensation? Because some of the parts such as lips and fingers have a lot of sensory detail than others; it's mainly for survival. Put simply, even if you have lost your arm your brain retains the sensation of that arm. Now you've lost your arm but the homunculus in your brain still retains that arm, so how does it adapt? When a brain doesn't trust itself but still tries to adapt, it uses some imperfect methods. The sensations of the missing left arm got merged with a neighbouring body part, so when I scratched Tushar's left cheek he felt it on his left arm that he reported to exist.

But then the brain would feel only what it experienced then why would he say that his hand was hideous. Let me explain, as I said our brain tries to fill up missing things, like, if you see a cat with half its body visually blocked, the brain will fill it up and see the whole cat. This general process is called insertion, the brain cells basically hate empty spaces and they fill it up.

The injury that Tushar received in the head in the accident damaged his optical lobe creating a blind spot in his vision which the other brain cells filled it up with the beings and made his left arm look hideous. This form of hallucination is called Bonnet Syndrome.

"In fact, many people suffer from this handicap, but only a few report it to doctors as they don't want anyone else to think that they are insane. Tushar here though, received the injury at a tender innocent age of three and thus reported it. And everyone here knows what happened when he did."

"But don't let that get to you Tushar, an American named James Thurber had the same handicap and he used it to become a famous cartoonist. So if your father asks me if you are fit enough to attend college, I assure you, you are more than ready with this information. I'm sorry I wasn't able to tell this to you in the beginning itself as I didn't know you were suffering from this then, but no harm is done even now. I wish you a great life ahead!"

"Thank you very much Dr. Saral." Tushar said.

And with that I left the premises immediately. My work was done.

Tushar will have a hard time accepting his situation now that he has finally understood it, but I am sure he'll manage in life. And I wish him the best!

Epilogue

Tushar's Narration

I won't linger around to tell you all the books I read or who my ancestors were or any unnecessary stuff. It has always been my motto to get straight to the point; it helps in my line of business, after all, I'm a cartoonist!

5

INTERNAL WOUNDS

by Maria Wynnckyj

I knew I needed to seek professional help, I truly thought I was going insane. My mind had started walking into a maze with no way out. My experience with survivor's guilt and being diagnosed with PTSD which was caused because of seeing a traumatic event occurring sent me over the edge. I needed to come back from that nightmare. I couldn't talk to people without breaking down when they would ask me how I was doing, I was only focused on my parents' wellbeing at that time as both my parents were lying in coma.

I sought help to try and stop seeing the movie being played over and over in my head as I watched both parents in total shock and disbelief. My parents were walking in front of me, then gone. My mind was reeling and spinning. I couldn't comprehend what had happened in an instant... Life changed so quickly... My horror of what I saw is something I cannot share. It's traumatic for me when I talk or write about it... I also feel my trauma will scar others who will read about it. Just remember one thing, time heals all, that movie of horror does subside as days pass, but the guilt never leaves. It's a matter of processing all the small things yourself and figuring out that in the end you did nothing wrong.

6

LOSS, HEALING AND LIFE

by Archana Natarajan

"Yay! I can see two pink lines. Come in, come in and see," Priya said excitedly, pulling Ajay's hand and ushering him inside the washroom.

"Okay, so tell me which is the correct one?" he asked in a puzzled manner while rubbing his sleepy eyes.'

"Look, this is the one that we have to concentrate on," she said pointing at the first pink line which had formed.

"The other pink line is called the control."

"So, what can we interpret?" he asked, still confused.

"That means, it is a positive test for pregnancy," she said and clicked a picture of the kit with her phone.

"Woah!!" he said while nudging her to put that stick down and keep the phone away.

She immediately followed suit and washed her hands.

He held her hand and suddenly made her twirl right there and held her in a tight embrace. Soon, they were snuggled up cosily under a blanket, wide awake at the crack of dawn, staring into each other's eyes and smiling wondering what the next course of action would be.

"We have a flight in to catch in just a few hours Pri, let's sleep now," he said, folding his arms around her, forcing her to sleep.

"I don't know whether to feel excited or nervous. I want to just go meet the doctor. Please take me home right now," Pri said.

"Come on, just try to get some sleep and then we will be on our way home soon. It is just a matter of a few hours," Ajay said assuring her.

Time flew fast and they were home in less than 8 hours.

The moment they sat in the cab, the first thing Ajay did was to book an appointment with a gynaecologist in the evening. Half an hour after the drive from the airport Priya started choking and coughing. Her throat was itching and she felt an irritating sensation that made her cough but each time, there was no sputum coming out. She coughed so much that she could barely breathe or talk. Ajay thought that she would have choked herself while popping in peanuts as the skin can sometimes get stuck to the throat and cause such irritation. He offered her warm water but that too didn't help. They closed the windows of the car and asked the driver to switch on the A.C in order to avoid the pollution from worsening her condition. Priya was feeling restless inside.

To make matters worse it was a bad day for the traffic leaving for the airport. The vehicles had piled near the toll gate and it would take them at least 3 hours to reach the clinic. All she wanted to do was get out of the cab and run to the doctor.

Finally, they were able to reach the hospital and meet the doctor before she left the clinic. The gynae was quite happy after seeing the picture she had taken of the positive pregnancy stick. But she was worried about the sudden bout of cough that Priya was having. On examination she found that her throat had a red rash inside which could be indicative of a bacterial infection. So, she wanted to do an early scan to see if the sac was visible after implantation. She asked Ajay to wait outside while she took Priya into the scanning room. Ajay squeezed Priya's hand as she pensively walked inside the scanning room with the doctor. Ajay was very restless as he waited outside for a long time.

The doctor came out with Priya in another 15-20 minutes and Priya had a look on her face that Ajay couldn't read.

"All good, Pri.?", he asked, stopping her midway before she could reach the doctor's chamber.

"Don't know, come, let's go," she said hurriedly and pulled him inside.

"Ajay, I couldn't see the gestational sac in the scan."

Ajay and Priya looked shocked and turned towards each other.

Seeing the quizzical look on their faces, the doctor continued, 'You are pregnant, Priya but I am unable to see the sac implanted into your uterus. There shouldn't be anything to worry about but I feel we should wait for another 10 days. Let's repeat the scan and we'll see as I feel it is too early to see a clear sac in the scan. Sometimes you can mess up your dates."

"Is there anything to worry about, doctor?" Pri asked in a nervous tone.

"No, I don't think so but I am worried about your throat infection. I am afraid I can't offer you any antibiotics as your pregnancy has just been confirmed. Try following simple steam inhalation and salt water gargle and you'll feel better. If you have any symptoms of severe cramps, pain, bleeding or high fever you'll report to me immediately," the gynae said and walked out of her clinic.

Ajay and Priya were her last patients for the day. Both of them sat outside her clinic absorbing what she had said. They did not know whether to feel happy or sad. Without thinking much they went home. As soon as they reached home they lay prostrate in front of the Almighty and prayed for everything to go well. Priya kept flipping through the scan report comments, trying to figure out what it meant. They did not want to reveal to their parents also until this was confirmed by the doctor. Ajay prepared a bowl of warm soup for her and they had simple khichdi for the night.

Priya was about to google search the terminologies written in the scan report when Ajay stopped her short and asked her to not do something like this as it would cause more stress and worsen her current condition. After the steam inhalation Priya felt better and stopped coughing. She went to bed early while Ajay did the unpacking. He did not want Priya to get stressed even a bit. At around 12 AM, after completing the work in the kitchen and tidying the house Ajay went to sleep when he saw Priya sleeping calmly like a baby occupying almost three-fourth of the bed. He went to push her aside slowly when he noticed that she was burning hot. He shook her slowly and asked her to get up and immediately checked her temperature, it was 101.5° F.

"Oh, my!! I am calling the doctor Pri," he said, asking her to lie down again. He called the doctor and explained to her the situation. She was also worried and immediately asked him to start on Dolo 650 as that was the only safe medications she could give first. She had also advised him to keep doing so every 5 hours and update her. Ajay didn't sleep well at all. Priya was burning hot with high fever and he was just praying all night that she should be alright. At around 5 AM her temperature shot up to 102.5. He called the doctor again and this time she asked him to give it every three hours. She was very kind enough to respond to all of Ajay's calls through the wee hours of the day. Priya's condition was not improving at all. Her temperature soared to 104 mid-morning and was touching 105° F when Ajay was rushing her to the clinic. She had started wheezing meanwhile but the doctor told her that the inhalers wouldn't work much even if she took them. She needed nebulization and hospitalization if it continued. While they were in the car Ajay also gave her an antibiotic as per doctor's advice. The gynae examined her and told her that if the fever persisted and her wheeze didn't settle, it would be of concern for the baby.

Priya was howling with sorrow as she sat in the car. Ajay was unable to console her but he acted strong, "Look Pri, nothing wrong has happened. If you cry like this your condition will worsen further. So please be calm and we'll pray that you are alright soon."

Priya tried to control her emotions but it wasn't easy to feel normal. She was so lethargic by the time they reached home that she even couldn't spend time to register what was happening with her. Ajay also tried to use a wet cloth pack on her forehead to get the fever down but Priya was just not feeling alright. She was burning hot. Only by the end of the day the fever came down a bit but her cough had not improved. Ajay was trying hard to juggle with the cooking and also looking after her. He took an off from work for a week so that he could be completely by her side.

By the next day there was some improvement in Priya's condition. After telling the doctor about the progress Ajay felt a little eased out. Priya also looked a bit better and was able to move around a bit in the house but she wasn't feeling normal. She had to collect some important documents from her office colleague so Ajay took her in the car halfway from their home where her colleague would come and give them to her. She informed her office about her health condition and told them that she might take leave for a couple of weeks. When they were returning home Pri started having a severe cramp on the left side, below her stomach. It was a kind of an ache which she had never felt before. She almost winced in pain when the car was turning on the curves. When they reached home, Priya immediately went and lay flat on the bed. She was howling as the pain was unbearable. Ajay was at his wits end seeing Priya's suffering.

"We will do something about this Pri. Please just hang on for a little while."

He spoke to the gynae and she told them to rush to the hospital immediately and she would be there in a while. It was close to 9 PM, when they reached the hospital. The doctor examined Priya's condition and did a scan immediately. They had just walked into their hospital in their pyjamas. Both had just their phone and wallet with them.

The doctor had a very grim look on her face when she saw Priya's scan images.

"Doctor, please tell me if everything is okay?" Priya asked in a pleading tone.

"No, dear. It doesn't look good. I can see the yolk sac, it is stuck in your tube, fallopian tube, look here." she said pointing at the screen.

"So, doctor? What does that mean?"

"It shows that the gestational sac has adhered to your fallopian tube, instead of the uterus wall and now it has started growing there. You have felt this pain because of a slight rupture that I can see on the scan.", she said and moved the probe deeply inside. It is an ectopic pregnancy Priya and I don't feel good about this.

"Ahhh, Priya cried as the probe moved deeply inside and also her heart just skipped a beat."

"I can see blood around the rupture. I don't think this will sustain. We need to put you in for an immediate surgery," the doctor said, keeping the probe down and helping Priya to get down from the bed.

Ajay was waiting outside when she took him separately and spoke to him.

"Look, this seems to be a case of an ectopic pregnancy, there is a tube burst as well. The yolk sac has stuck to her fallopian tube instead of the uterus wall and the baby has no space to grow further. The rupture is the cause of the pain and I could also see minimal bleeding. We need to operate on her immediately otherwise it will be too late. She can also go into a coma if we don't take immediate action," the gynae explained in a crisp clear voice and went aside to make important calls to get the other doctors of her team on board for the surgery. The nurses were instructed within minutes and there were three nurses who had surrounded Ajay and Priya in moments.

Ajay took Priya aside and squeezed her hand tight. She looked pale and shocked. Ajay's hand was cold and he was trembling. He gathered himself and asked Priya to hand over her phone and wallet. "All that matters to me right now is that I want you healthy and alive. Anything for your life right now Pri." he said holding her tightly. Then he told her to go with the nurse while he would be doing the admission formalities. Priya was just not able to understand what was happening. She had no clue about what an ectopic pregnancy was and she was not even clear what was happening to her. She was admitted and had to be immediately changed into an OT gown. Ajay came in soon along with her gynaecologist. Priya just couldn't take this anymore.

"My baby, doctor. I don't want to lose my baby,' she wailed and hot tears burst from her eyes."

"Look Priya, this is an emergency situation. Your tube has ruptured, if we do not operate it is a matter of your life. Unfortunately, we have to remove your fallopian tube. Dear, if you cry more your BP will fluctuate and we cannot give anaesthesia to you. It will be a simple laparoscopic surgery, hardly going to take long and the stitches will heal soon. You can walk home in just one day."

"What about my future pregnancy?" Priya asked.

"I have personally handled many cases where ectopic cases with one tube have resulted in natural conception in the future. One tube is enough for conception, yes with 50% chances but that's a lot when I treat cases with 0% chances also. Even one fimbriae is enough for the next conception. Please trust me, it will happen and you will be alright. Now, please steady yourself as we need to take you to the OT." the doctor said in a very reassuring and calm tone.

It helped calm the situation in the room. As Priya was wheeled to the OT with drips hanging from her arms Ajay felt his eyes clouding with tears as he watched her go. He walked up and down until the surgery was done. He saw Priya back in the recovery room where she just opened her eyes and saw him before she was sleeping again. They gave her just a few drops of water. Ajay sat there waiting for her to be conscious again. It was almost the early hours of the morning of the next day when Priya was brought back to the room. Ajay held her hand and they both sobbed. Ajay was glad that Priya's life was saved on time but also sad about their loss. It took weeks for Priya to recover and Ajay handled this all alone. He had to call up their respective families and tell them about this sudden shocking incident. Both parents were in shock and Priya's parents flew in immediately.

Priya was slowly recovering from her surgery but the pain in her heart increased day by day. Passing each day was a nightmare. Ajay and her parents tried to keep her occupied but she was unable to divert her mind anywhere. She felt an instant attachment with the baby the day she had found she was pregnant. The doctor tried to convince her by telling her that it was just 6 weeks and she shouldn't be too worried as her health was also coming back to normal but Priya just couldn't get convinced. She would be talking to Ajay about something and suddenly start crying remembering the incident or wake up with a nightmare and start crying. Ajay hid all his unhappiness and put up a brave shoulder for her to cry on. If he became weak in front of her she would never come out of this grief. Ajay had to resume work soon but Priya was not in a state to get back to work. She took an extended leave citing reasons for recovery. Her parents had also left for their hometown after Priya's health had recovered. They wanted Ajay and Priya to take it slow and heal slowly. They both needed time to heal their wounds. The shock was more than the wound.

One evening over a cup of coffee Priya sobbed to Ajay and asked, "Why me Ajay? Why did this happen only to me? Why did it affect us in such a harsh way?"

"I am unable to get any answers. I have been reading a lot about ectopic pregnancy but nothing seems to be clear. My symptoms just don't fit in," she added.

"I told you not to read about all this online. We have already got an answer from the doctor and she has told you everything in detail. It just happened. Maybe it was because of the infection or something that causes the sac to stay there in the tube. Our case was unusual but tell me what can we do about it now?" Ajay said, trying to convince Priya.

"I am not convinced. I want closure to this; I want my answers, Ajay and for that I will go to any extent," Priya said in a firm tone.

"Do whatever it takes to make yourself feel better my dear, I am there to support you. All I care about is that your life was saved and my future is only safe if you are with me. Together we can create our future and there is hope. It will happen and my heart is filled with hope. Didn't you hear about the various cases the doctor has attended to. I felt very positive but Pri please, I request you, please, don't ask the- Why me? Question again." Ajay said with optimism in his voice.

"Okay," Priya said and fell silent.

"But......."

She was stopped short by Ajay as the next moment he hugged her tight and let her sob in her arms. He was taking in all the grief only to help her feel better.

Priya was not letting this go and it was driving her into a depressive phase. Upon the strict instructions from her doctor she had to resume work otherwise the doctor had warned Ajay that she would be slipping into depression soon. She had left doing all the normal things that she did before. Ajay coaxed her to start driving again and also forced her to cook some amazing dishes that she was an expert at. Slowly, once she went back to work she felt a little normal but these thoughts kept running in her mind.

A talk by a distant aunt about them planning a family soon and taunting Priya indirectly brought all those sad memories back to her mind. That nosy aunt had actually rubbed salt on her wounds and the repercussion was not what Ajay was prepared to take. Pri was not her usual self that day. Those sad thoughts had also made her doubt about the support Ajay was to her. It was a day of multiple discussions and arguments that ended only in sobs and sniffles. They couldn't do anything productive that day.

"Look Priya, you are going down the wrong path. It has been months to that incident now and you are still stuck there. I have moved on and I am hoping for a positive future. If you can't make the attempt to get out of this phase then at least don't pull me with you inside this dark well. You are spiralling towards depression and if you keep searching for answers, you will not get one." Ajay said sternly. He had to be rude and blunt because the doctor had warned him about this phase that Priya could go into. He was told to be very supportive yet be very stern with her when it came to sad thoughts. He was unable to control himself after the outburst he had seen from Priya.

Priya stared at him in silence and walked out of the house for some fresh air. Ajay, just couldn't hold back his emotions anymore. He was done playing the part of acting normal. With a heavy heart he sat down and waited for Priya to come home. She was definitely normal when she came home but very cold. He was searching for that warmth in her after that day. Weeks passed this way but Priya never expressed her feelings again to him. It took time but Priya was slowly getting back to normalcy.

It was pricking Ajay a lot, so he planned a short outing for them so that they could take steps towards healing their relationship as well. Priya agreed to it easily and was very happy during the trip. While Ajay was driving the car, Priya was busy reading up articles on ectopic pregnancy and the emotions that the woman/ couple has to go through post that. She was shocked that there was so much about it online. She was reading out to Ajay while he was driving. He told her, "Look Priya, we are not going there again."

"No, it is nothing about me going into a depressive phase but I feel there are so many women who go through this. I am not alone and my feelings are not false. What all I have gone through post the loss has been written about and well documented. There is so much scientific data on Ajay that I am very very motivated to find out more about it," Priya said reassuring him.

"Sure, go ahead but please, please, promise me you'll not go into that phase again. I can't handle it Pri. I don't have the courage to. I want a good future with you. Let us hope for the best", Ajay said, feeling glad that he could see a positive outlook in Priya.

The next few days Priya spent in reading many scientific articles and a lot of posts on Instagram and Facebook when she put the hashtag #ectopicpregnancy. That's when a UK based website called 'Ectopic pregnancy Trust'(ETPT) popped up in her search. This trust was doing everything possible to help women who had gone through ectopic pregnancy and also creating an awareness about the priority on the mental health and well-being of such women. There were many stories where women had shared their experiences. After reading and checking their website in detail, Priya was inspired to do some collaborative work with them. She, as an individual, had Ajay and her family to support her in such terrible times but there was no one for many women who would be able to get the troubled women out of the sad phase they were going through. There were psychologists and experts in the panel along with volunteers. They also organized fundraisers (charity events), marathons, meet-ups and also counselling sessions for all the women affected by it and whoever approached them for help.

Feeling inspired, Priya wrote to them and discussed in detail about her story. She also did her background research that such things were never spoken about or discussed in India. There will be many women who would want to hide about these problems and wouldn't gather courage to share their feelings with anyone, as a result those who had unsupportive families would slip into mental health problems. She proposed a plan to take the help of Ectopic Pregnancy Trust, UK and build a similar platform for women in India. She roped in her gynaecologist first. She was very happy to see Priya back to her normal and was very much helpful in giving her data points to present to the trust back in the UK. Since Priya needed funds to rope in a psychologist, a counsellor and also a data entry operator, she requested them to grant her an initial seed fund. The credentials of her gynaecologist and the interest that Priya had shown had impressed the ETPT Trust and they invited her to the UK to be a spokesperson along with her gynaecologist. Her doctor was very enthusiastic and together they presented important data points about the Indian scenario. They were appreciated by thousands of women who had come to attend the meeting and also were backed up by the scientists and clinicians from the UK who were on board. The seed fund was granted to set up an 'ETPT' Trust in India and they were sent home with encouraging words and brilliant ideas. Before returning home, Priya and her doctor also participated in the marathon organized by them as a part of a fundraiser programme.

Priya started working on setting up the trust as soon as she was back. She and Ajay took a lot of pain in finding a small office space for this trust, roped in the other doctors and also took help from close friends to become volunteers. The gynaecologist spread in a word in her community as well so that more women could reach out to the helpline number they had started. The website and Instagram posts were a hit as soon as they were rolled out. The helpline number soon started flooding with calls from women who really wanted to seek help pertaining to counselling and also clinically. Slowly, things were falling into place and Priya was feeling highly motivated to do more for this. Her efforts were much appreciated as they also participated in a scientific conference and spread the word. They also organized awareness programmes through Facebook live sessions so that everyone in the world/ country could participate. After taking some help from the USF foundation they also organized a fundraiser 5km Walkathon. It garnered a lot of appreciation and Priya also wrote a column for the newspaper. Slowly, many women wanted to volunteer and whatever money they had earned was enough. Ajay had been a constant support system for Priya throughout this journey. He was very happy to see the zeal back in her and he was seeing the healed version of his Pri now.

Priya had planned a fun and awareness event for Women's Day online when multiple women had joined their Facebook live session that day. Post her session she was feeling very exhausted and wanted to sleep early so that she could go to work on time the next day. They ordered food for the night and Priya went to sleep early. She was woken up at 5 am with a dull ache in her stomach and a kind of nauseous feeling. She tip-toed into the bathroom without waking up Ajay and took the kit out to test. Her eyes filled with tears as she saw those two pink lines again.

"Ajayyyyyyyyy, she shouted and jolted him from his sleep."

***

Research and several studies have shown that early-stage pregnancy loss like miscarriages and ectopic pregnancies have a tremendous impact on the mental health of women resulting in post-traumatic stress, depression and anxiety. These adverse situations take a toll on a woman's mental health and in turn deeply affect their relationship with their spouse and other family members and also affecting their quality of life with some worse cases resulting in suicide. Women are often unnecessarily blamed and held responsible for such incidents over which sometimes women have no control. Lack of empathy and support causes the grief to worsen affecting mental and physical healing. It is very essential for the family and close friends to offer emotional support and help women seek proper medical advice which will help them overcome the loss, get over the grief and help them in healing in a better way.

7

WHEN THE HEART FEELS YOUR SONG

by Valerie Hernandez

Sometimes I wish I could switch places with him. Sometimes I wish it was me that this was happening to. I took his hand, squeezed it tightly, and he gave me a smile, as he continued to listen to the testimonies of other patients.

We met one summer, many years ago. I was a young student with a lot of part-time jobs, saving as much as possible for college. He was a promising young musician. A talented guitarist and singer. Tall, handsome, with an intense personality and a look that melted you like butter over warm bread.

It was love at first sight. I was the assistant to the festival organizers, he played that day. He got my phone number and one day he started writing to me. That's how it all began: messages full of love, songs and poetry. Many gifts and flowers. Endless romanticism like a Beatles song. Emotion, pyrotechnics and magic, like any relationship at the beginning. Going to the movies, accompanying him to his concerts and long walks in the park with a coffee, watching the sunset and talking about this and that.

As time went by, we decided to live together. He was already earning a lot of money and traveling a lot. His tours were normally over 40 days. I was already at college and looking forward to his calls every night, to hear his voice and all the stories of the incredible places that he visited, all the people he met and how he filled stadiums, with people shouting his name and chanting his songs. I always missed him and loved him a lot. We always supported each other's projects, we were always there for each other.

However, fame and fortune came at a cost. The constant pressure from the label, his manager, the Booking Agency and sponsors, as well as the constant trips month after month: tours all over Europe and Australia; the United States, Canada and Latin America. Led him to rampant drug and alcohol use. Parties and more parties. Fans and more fans. I didn't know if I could bear that. For me the cost was too much.

We parted ways on a cold February morning, I discovered him with another woman in bed, after a night of partying. It was painful, it was intense and it was very sad. I threw some things in his face and we said others that we wanted to forget. I took my stuff and had no choice but to return to my parents. I had no friends, no job, no place to live, and didn't know what to do. At that moment I felt lonelier than ever, sadder than ever and in a thousand pieces. I felt lost. I had already seen our future together, between the warm and sweet kisses; his arms so comforting and safe; his words full of love and promises; everything seemed viable. But now, I didn't know how to put the pieces back together, how to get up, and how to get on with my life. He was happy traveling the world, accumulating awards and successes; and sleeping with a different woman every night. And I... I just wanted to die.

After a year I managed to put myself back together again. I graduated from college, got a good job, moved to New York, and met a new man. He made me forget everything bad about my previous relationship, but especially, he made me regain my faith in love. A couple of years later, we had a beautiful beach wedding, bought an apartment, and adopted a dog. I was promoted at my job and life seemed good, until I got a call.

Eleven years have passed, since I last heard from him. But that morning, his manager called to tell me that he had had a very bad episode of depression and tried to kill himself. Now he was admitted to a well-known hospital in Los Angeles and he wanted me to travel to be with him; because only I know him, only I understand him, only I can bring him that peace and security that nothing and no one has ever been able to give him.

I was shocked on the other end of the line, as my assistant reminded me that everyone was already waiting in the conference room. I apologized and told him that I couldn't give him an answer right now, I was working and needed time to think about it. We hung up and although my presentation went very well, my mind wandered the rest of the day and night. While eating sushi with my husband, I couldn't stop thinking about that phone call and about him, my first love. How he was with me when my father died of cancer, how he helped me pay for college and how whenever I needed him, he was with me, regardless of whether he was in Malaysia, Stockholm or Mexico City, even through a screen, he was always with me and I thought it was fair to do the same for him.

I asked for a couple of days off at work and lied to my husband. I took the first available flight to Los Angeles. When I arrived, his manager picked me up and we headed to the hospital. He was unconscious with a tube stuck in his throat, many machines around him and the sound of his heart on the monitor was constant. Like when I hugged him very tight and that sound calmed me down, it reminded me of home. I took his hand and spent most of the day there with him.

The next morning, he was awake and ready for discharge. We went to his apartment on the beach. He insisted a lot on me to stay. In the end, I managed to be with him for just over three months. I managed to work remotely and balance my work with his care. Of course, the first days were very difficult. The doctors' instruction was that he had to have a routine, eat healthy, exercise, sunbathe at least 20 minutes a day and sleep 8 hours. I was always searching YouTube for vegan recipes and yoga studios near home, because he had decided to adopt this lifestyle derived from a trip to Tibet.

Some days we would walk barefoot on the beach, smiling at each other at every opportunity and looking at each other with love, as if time had never passed by us. Other days were difficult, because it took a long time to find the perfect drug combination. Some medications anesthetized him, he could not write or compose. Not even have a normal conversation. Others made him very irritable, made him gain weight, lose his hair or cause acne. His libido completely disappeared. We even tried marijuana and sometimes that helped, but others didn't.

We had a blackboard in the kitchen, to write down everything: from his routine and medications, to what phrases to say to him when he had a bad day. Living with a person with depression was not as easy as I thought. I had no idea and I thought it would be like any other disease, but the reality was different. He had good days, in which we had a lot of fun, went to the movies, took long motorcycle rides and made me remember the past, but especially rethink the future; a future with him.

Other days weren't so good. I couldn't get him out of bed or get him to eat. He moved in black and white around the apartment. I felt helplessness and despair. Then we discovered a support group not far from his apartment. Every Saturday at 4pm we would hear testimonials from people living with schizophrenia, depression, anxiety, and more. This also allowed me to meet their families and caregivers, but above all to understand more about this. Of course, he hated going. But he did it for me, he knew that I needed it and that it was important to me.

I discovered that the opposite of depression is not being happy all the time but living. Talking with the patients' families and caregivers gave me encouragement, ideas, and ways to deal with him and the situation we lived in at home. However, it was time for me to return to New York. As much as I would have liked to stay by his side and take care of him; I had a life on the other side of the country that I just couldn't leave.

I went back to New York and to my life. Time passed, but as much as I tried to insert myself again, I couldn't. My mind and my heart were on the west coast with him. His manager hired nurses, cleaning staff, and a food delivery service. But he was lonely and constantly calling me. All of these, along with the pressure of work and my marriage, because we were looking to start a family, was too much for me. I started to lose weight quickly and had insomnia. I felt a lot of stress and a very strong pain in my heart. I didn't know whether to make that sacrifice for him. If he deserved it, after so many years and after what he did to me.

One day I decided to cancel my appointment at the fertility clinic. I also cancelled my afternoon meetings and decided to walk around New York. Enjoy the autumn breeze, buy a coffee, and sit in the park watching people walk hand in hand, skate, smile, and listen to some music. So, I decided to go back to California with him. I didn't belong here, I belonged by his side. I felt a very strong burden for him, I felt responsibility, but above all love and that, moved me.

That night I waited for my husband to give him the news of our separation. He took it badly and threatened to take everything away from me. But I packed all my stuff, quit my job overnight, and took a flight to LA. He couldn't drive so I took an Uber and went to his apartment. He was waiting for me at the entrance with a huge bouquet of red roses, as in the past and as he always had. With a beautiful smile and a sparkle in his eyes.

I heard a song coming from within. Like when we lived together. He hugged me very tightly and kissed me very tenderly. I knew that things would not be easy and the relationship would never be like before. But I decided that I was going to do it; I was going to fight for his life. Because I loved him and wanted him to live.

POEMS

8

UNSWEETENED ANXIE-TEA

When the butterflies in your stomach turn into bees,
Holding up two fingers is the only known peace.
When you break free from the cage but are still incarcerated
in the sky.
And "I am fine" becomes your favourite lie.

When the silence becomes deafening and you find chaos in
the calm,
And every thought disturbs you like an annoying alarm.
It's like being followed by a voice who whispers self-doubt,
And fills your mind with thoughts that won't get out.

The voice of your insecurities and fears
Echoes in your mind, not just your ears
And leaves your face concealed with dried tears,
Making some nights feel longer than years.

To feel nothing at all or be filled with emotion
Like dying of drought while drowning in the ocean.
And reassurances like "it's all in your head" make it worse
Invalidating how we feel just adds to the curse.

by Dhwanie Shetty

9

A PAUSE IN A BAD ROUTINE

I wake up,
with a bad headache,
I don't want to leave my bed;
I'd rather sleep forever.

I look in the mirror,
I hate it,
I look like a car crash.
What a disgusting view.

I look fat,
I look ugly,
I look dead.
What a disgrace.

Kill me.
No, don't.
I want to live,
but I wish I were dead.

I am fighting with myself,
every day,
Which side will have control over me today?
The good or the bad?

Overthinking is my breakfast,
questioning everything, my lunch,
Smoking half a pack a day, my snack,
And having a mental breakdown, my dinner.

Today was a good day though;
Today I didn't cry,
Today I reached for help;
Today the good side won.

by Mara Martins

10

BAD TRIP

I'm at a party.
I don't feel well.
My heart starts pounding really fast.
My breaths get shorter and faster.
My throat starts aching. I'm trembling.
Sweat is dripping off my face.
It's so cold.
Chills are climbing up my back.
It's so hot in here.
I can't breathe.
I want to puke.
Stop cramping, belly.
I am breathing too fast.
No air enters my lungs.
My throat hurts.
My lungs hurt.
I feel dizzy.
My hands around my neck.
Stop breathing.
It hurts.
My sight is blurry.
I feel really dizzy.

Help.
I can't breathe.
Stop it.
Please.
I am shaking.
I stopped breathing.
I fainted.
I woke up.
I'm exhausted.
Another panic attack.
I want to go home now.

by Mara Martins

11

LOVE THEM

In a society where functioning
without failure is key
The hearts of thousands of people
Don't stand the constant pressure
Their brains just stop working
their souls implode
leaving a dark and cold void
A breeze of bitterness and sadness
enters their bodies
creating depressed creatures
seeking for help and warmth
aching for an embrace of security and love

If you see a broken soul
A dead brain
And a pressured heart
Give them some warmth
Guide them to find themselves again
Give them security
Love them

by Mara Martins

12

AM I MENTAL?

There's something inside
Something dark that wants to hide
Ruling in the shadows of my mind
Making me crazy – a cure I can't find

Coursing through my nerves
Through all the twists and turns
Anger - on a platter served
Sanity dumped with every swerve

Finally it's too much
The weight is too heavy – I'm crushed
Weight of sadness – inside, hushed
Weight of tears – aside, brushed

I'm tired of fake laughs and smiles
Emotion waiting – a ready missile
Shooting over miles and miles
Erupting fire from a pile of lies

But what's the use of telling the truth?
Any illness it doesn't cure
"Insane" reads my label, writing jagged and rude
Ousted by all – the young and youth

"I'm mental!" I wanna shout
But I'm not insane – that there's no doubt
I am sick – but I ain't gonna pout
Gonna win this challenge and take the right route

I'm going to win by taking the right route
Because "I'm mental."

No shame in saying it out loud

by Nehal Gandhi

13

CREATION IN DESTRUCTION

Have you ever felt
an indefinable ache
and you don't even know
where it is coming from?
You feel like you're a
ticking time bomb
and you're on the verge
of jumping off the cliff
of self-destruction.

Then you pick up your pen
holding on to it tight
as if your life
depends on it
and you cling with all
your remaining strength
like it would save you
from sinking in the
quicksand of your
internal turbulence.

Why is it that
destruction and creation
go together,
sealed by fate,
betrothed for life?
Why is it that
one cannot survive
without the other?

What is it about destruction
that makes it diabolically beautiful?

by Yohan Acosta

14

DEAR WARRIOR

Caffeine nights to sustain daily fights
Plant wilts and you wait
For the shades of water to show
The anxiety tiptoes to bed
You decide to fight a battle you never led
Wounds bleed open each time
harsh words are showered
The pills stitch them
But never heals truly and makes it a burrow
Pills can't put you to bed but gentle words can
Shades of water don't settle for land

Dear warrior,
You're stronger than you think you are
The toughest chapters made you braver
and here you are
Someday you'll have the smiling sun
and the flowers which won't bother
And to these warriors
the countrymen will support
Let this no more be a subject latter
Because mental health matters

Dear warrior,
Hold on to hope and keep going
You're the endless and fearless river
that keeps flowing

by Aishwarya Shukla

15

DRY PILLOW, WARM AND MELLOW

Dry pillow, warm and mellow
I reminisce a hundred thousand pasts
as I lay on it facing west
To days when once it was soaked
in tears as warm as my wretched blood
when the world kept cutting my strings
and I struggled to stand under the sun
when I'd had friends who weren't friends
when I'd wish for only one person
and I'd rather be hated than pitied
Of waking days dosed on fake strength
coping on stupid attention and validation
yet going deeper into endless nights
every single night
screaming into my pillows, yanking my hair out
praying to never see tomorrow again

Dry pillow, warm and mellow
I reminisce a hundred thousand presents
as I lay on it facing east
To the girl who stands on her own
fighting no longer with herself

but for herself
seeking validation now rather from her own soul
drenched in sunlight and moonlight

I see you
I stand facing you in the mirror
And I am proud of you
The sails were rough the journey more
but you withstood storms and wreckages
and now you rule the ocean
the raging waters within your mind

by Athena Thiyam

16

EVERYTHING WILL BE ALRIGHT

A war with oneself is the cruellest one of them all
The silent insanity and a constant state of unease drives you
up the wall
It follows you through thick and thin and creeps up to you
It comes and goes away and leaves you in a haze of grey and
blue

Frenetic cries drown in the depths of an anxious mind
And no matter how hard you try, it keeps playing back like
on rewind
You start to wonder how you are still breathing under this
skin
You want to rest even if it's for a minute whatever thought
that lies therein

It's the dull cloud of gloom that hangs on you even on a
sunlit day
It's learning that not all people are poetries the hard way
Maybe that's what life's all about; all the lessons we learn
Until the light comes and gets us all, to live gloriously in this
world eternally

When you finally find a salvage, you become a survivor
But when you truly start believing in yourself
That's when you become a warrior
Keep in mind it's always the small steps that count
Wading through the madness and chaos

You are here
Right now

Breathe
Just breathe

by Ishwari Salunke

17

FIGHT WITH THE MONSTERS INSIDE

I can feel the monsters
Hear the chanting devils
See the demons chasing me
Trying to get to me

I open my eyes and realize
that they're all in my head
Seemingly palpable yet so intangible
I know that they're real
The world can say whatever it wants
but I know the truth

I don't know what to do
Do I just give up?
Succumb to these devils and their power?
Are they really stronger than me?

They stop me from doing the things I like
They tell me nothing is going to be alright
I can see them holding me down
Are they really holding me though?

Again, it's all in my head, and so real
But now, every day
I feel their grasp get a little loose
Every day, I try to fly higher and fail and try again
I guess that this is all it takes

To keep trying each day to survive
Rise from the flames
that demons light for me, like a phoenix
I think they've left me now, don't feel them anymore
Perhaps I killed them or time destroyed them
I lived through nonetheless

by Malay Mundra

18

GENUINE OR NOT

Many people have referred to me
As a man who lightened heavy hearts around him
But not many know the true me
As a man who faked a new personality around him

And that's how I am
A fake projection
Faking new personalities, emotions and feelings
Have I now become like a salesman
Who says anything to make out his dealings?

I have until now been that kind of a guy
To whom his popularity and reputation mattered the most
A guy who was a good, selfless, helpful, kind person
Amongst this, the real me seems to have become
a forgotten ghost

And living this life again every day
as I came to school in the morning
I saw this new face looming across the class
A new admission it seemed, a face glittering with life
So bright, like a reflecting glass

His eyes were of different colours
a combination of red and blue
And he carried a diary in his hands
holding events of his life that were true
Due to my 'reputation' across the place
the teacher asked him to sit beside me
Hoping that I'd help him fit in
while I hoped I could be free

But I had this reputation to maintain you know
something I'd never give up
And so I waived to him as he sat beside me
and the class broke up
He had nice and firm vocal cords
a reliable persona surrounding
and we talked of academics
sports and whatnot
to his pleasurable founding

A little time into the conversation
suddenly his persona changed
Where the firmness existed
and reliability he became a bit deranged
He spoke now in a quiet squeaking voice
leaving me astounded
He introduced himself again but
with a different name than before
his shoulders now a bit more grounded

He told me that there were two people
living in his single body
What we'd call the identity disorder
They tried to keep up with the society
while working twice
While things went back to order

He told me that they wrote in a diary
about everything and every conversation
So that there was no confusion
and the other could keep up with information
And they even tried to match preferences
so as to avoid inconvenience to the other
and this huge amount of surprising information
left me with a tickling sensation

For here was I a single whole guy
who faked different non-genuine personalities
and here were these two in one completely
different people trying to be a single entity
If it wasn't before my eyes
I might not have believed it at all I'm definitely sure
It might be fate knocking on my doors
that I met a complete opposite of me
talking about his daily chores

And this is where I learned
that I shouldn't be such a person
who faked everything about him and wasn't genuine
For there are people who can't do such things
and yet they try their best,
These unfortunate people
who have a little creative fuzzy brain
that doesn't allow them to rest

So be thankful to god and a little alert
and on a constant lookout
Stay genuine and stay least cared
about what others think of you
Be healthy and mentally strong
and genuinely wholesome
For every genuine person in this world
turns out to be intriguing and awesome

by A Low Kick

19.

HIDDEN DARKNESS

"Be yourself," they say
"Show us who you are"
I will show you a darkness you didn't expect
a pain you never imagined
a brokenness that goes deeper than you know
for this is what lies beyond my walls
this is what lies beneath my layers of stone
if I am going to show you who I am
this is what you are going to see
it will surprise you
for it is so different from what you are seeing now
so when you ask me to show you who I am
make sure you are ready
for what you are going to see

by Rebecca Hilliard

20

I HOPE IT DOESN'T SCARE YOU AWAY

I hope it doesn't scare you away
If you get to know me you'll get to know my pain
I hope it doesn't scare you away
For it scares me
I don't understand it
I just know it's deep
It reaches to the far corners of my soul
Entangling everything in its tendrils
So that I am lost in it
I am intertwined with its grip
I don't see where I begin and it ends
I don't know if I'll ever get out
But if you are going to get to know me
you are going to get to know it
I hope it doesn't scare you away

by Rebecca Hilliard

21

IF I TELL YOU, WILL YOU LISTEN?

I am broken
I have been overlooked
misunderstood
neglected
and I have blamed myself
but it is not my fault
I am not tainted that people should abandon me
I am not marred that I deserve to be alone
No
I was not given the chance to grow
to become myself
even to find myself
and in not being given the chance to grow
I have missed myself completely
I conformed
fit into the mold
out of fear
fear of being rejected, abandoned
but there is nothing like the feeling of loneliness
that comes from not being known
nothing goes deeper than that
nothing hurts more than that

for it is this kind of isolation that kills the soul
it is this kind of isolation that sucks the life out of you
so that you are walking around dead
I do not want to be walking around dead
I didn't know there was an alternative
or at least what the alternative was
I want people to know me
I want people to know I am broken
I do not want to hide anymore
If I tell you, will you listen?

by Rebecca Hilliard

22

UNDER THE MASK

Who am I under the mask?

There have been a lot of masks going up recently
Figuratively and literally
Wherever we go these days
people are wearing literal masks

It's strange and unnerving
We can thank Covid for that
But I wonder how many people
are wearing emotional masks as well?

I know I used to all the time
I still do

When I'm out in public
it doesn't feel safe
to show people who I really am
I'm constantly trying to do and say things
that will make them happy

It's because I'm afraid of rejection
I wear my mask because I am afraid of rejection
I think that if people really knew who I was
they wouldn't want to be with me anymore

That's a message I received from childhood
and it still affects me to this day
I wonder if childhood messages
are the reasons we all wear masks

We're adults now
but still we feel scared like little kids inside
and we think that wearing our masks will protect them
But I'm learning that it's important to take off that fake mask

I'm learning that some people will stay
Some people will accept me and love me as I am
I'm learning that some people want to know the real me
And it feels so amazing to be wanted and known and loved

It's quite healing actually
I think it's going to heal those harmful childhood messages
I've been living with
I am worth knowing and loving
and so are YOU

There are people who will want to know the real you
People who will love who you are under your mask

It's safe to take it off sometimes
It's safe to show people who you are

Maybe not everyone,
but someone who is safe and loving
My wish for us is that we can all find someone
who wants to know who we are under our masks

by Rebecca Hilliard

23

WHAT IS LIFE IF YOU CAN'T DREAM?

I can feel the sun beating into my back
As I ponder what my day will be like
What my life will be like
What my life has become

I did not see it going this way
When a child dreams about their future
They do not see it going this way

So I ponder
When I think about the future now
I am afraid to dream about anything else
Because of how far off I was the first time
I don't want to be that far off again
That disillusioned again

But what is life if you can't dream?
What is life if you can't hope?

At this point
I'm not even sure what I would dream of
I stopped doing that a long time ago

And have just spent my time focusing on surviving
But to survive is not to live
I want to live
I want to be bold enough to dream again

Will I get crushed in the process?
Maybe
Or maybe
life could be more than I ever thought
it could be

by Rebecca Hilliard

24

WHO AM I?

Who am I?

That's a question I like to avoid
That's a question I don't know the answer to

Who am I?

I know I've been hiding for a long time
Hiding behind a façade that I've perfected
I know I don't want to hide anymore
I want to be seen

I'm not often seen
In a family where perfection is expected
it's hard to be seen
What would happen if I were to show you
Who I truly am?

Would you accept me?
Reject me?
Would you be disappointed in what you see?

For I am not perfect
I am actually broken
I am hurting
I have lost my way
and I'm not sure if it's ok to tell you that

But I've found that I like myself a lot more
lost in the brokenness
than I do striving for perfection

I think I am beginning to find myself here
I spend a long time refusing to look inside myself
I was afraid of what was in there
I was afraid of who I was

As I look inside, yes it is dark
Yes, it is scary
But it is also beautiful

There are beautiful parts of me I didn't know existed
It's funny how when you admit you are broken
you start to see yourself for the first time
It's funny how when you realize you have nothing
you start to find what you've been looking for the whole time

I am broken,
I've gotten lost
and I am filled with shame
But I will not hide anymore
It's time to show you who I really am
A beautiful mess of darkness and light
fighting to find my way

Who am I?
I am not perfect
I am a living, breathing, dreaming
thinking, feeling like a human being

And I am finding in these imperfections
there is more to me
that I ever thought there could be

by Rebecca Hilliard

25

I STAY ALIVE FOR YOU

I envy you,
I envy your innocence

What is it like to live without darkness?
To have a clear mind?
To not have to fight to stay alive?

I'm glad you don't know what it's like
As much as I want to be understood
I'm glad you don't understand
I'm glad the only times you've seen it
are when you've felt it from me

I hate that you've had to experience even that
I like seeing the joy in your eyes
I like that you are free

Escaping my pain means
increasing yours
I can't do that to you
The darkness, it is endless
But I stay alive for you

by Rebecca Hilliard

26

SUICIDE AWARENESS

There are two voices calling
one says stay, the other go

Which will I listen to?
There is one that is stronger
More alluring
Tempting
Darker

It pulls on my heart strings
whispers in my ear
calls to me
I want to follow it
I want to go
it promises freedom
it promises peace
I've never known peace
I want to go

but there's that other voice
barely audible
It says to stay
It says, "What if it's wrong?"
"What if leaving is a mistake?"

It keeps me here
for now
For if you are going to leave you must be sure
You must be aware of what you're giving up
You must have tried everything else first

Should I stay or should I go?

This is the question that haunts me

by Rebecca Hilliard

27

HOLD ON

Someone told me, there's a million ways to die
and I think maybe once upon a time
we've all held them in our minds
The world, it's held on pretty little strings
And sometimes it all just feels like
such a fragile thing

She thinks no one hears, oh how she cries
Every day seems another bad luck ride
I know your heart feels like ice
but you can't take this back
Please think twice

There is this boy with stars in his eyes
He is blinded, the world is too bright
He holds a current just under his skin
His hands always shake
He can't hold it in

Does she believe that it gets better?
How do I show him it will all be okay?
This is a life I have seen; I have lived

and if you think no one cares, think again
To all the boys with scars in their eyes
and girls with ice in their minds
I'll give you this one bit of advice
You can't fix the past, so please live the present
And I promise one day you'll be alright

by Keegan Cockin

28

I AM MENTAL, I AM ILL

It grows darker inside everyday
I cannot live and am too afraid to say
I feel pain scribbling over my tissues
They say, "I got some serious issues"
I have to take those bitter pills
But I think I'm just adding money to my bills
A demon creates a void in my debilitate body
He rules over me and I can't do anything
Proves to be a nasty master as he enslaves me
I am blind and I cannot see
I am naive and stuck to become dumb
My thoughts make me mad and numb
He took an advantage of my situation
Everyday I feel near my last breath
He pricks me with a dangerous needle
Each day to me is like a new death
I am sick and tired of handling my pain
I am sick when people call me insane
I decided to give up and prove them right
But when I contemplated on one lonely night
I realised that inside me was so much light
I am ashamed that I didn't try to cure it

I am ashamed because I decided to quit
But now no more silence
Enough of the terrible violence
I am ready and armed to defeat the demon
Which surrounds my thoughts
and makes them negative
I am disturbed and my emotions are spilled
I am mental, I am ill
If fighting back is the cost, I will

by Vidhi Jain

29

I FEEL

I feel.
I feel blue, I feel red,
I feel gray, I feel pain,
but mostly black.

Do you feel?
My dear depression,
I don't think you do,
I think you're empty of;
love, anger, pain, fear, joy,
And you're making me miss the validation
Of how it felt when I could love
And be loved,
Hate, and be loathed.

So inject your insecurities into my bloodstream
And dilute the sadness in my veins,
And I am not really there anymore,
Because I only exist when I feel
And you take the pain away,
Leaving me a blank abyss of nothing.

Until you leave again,
And I am reborn
In a hundred drops of saltwater
And a thousand cherry blossoms
And a million rays of sunlight
And a single smile that life steals
From me, as I sip my coffee on the terrace
And butterflies prance by my hydrangea.

by Despina Sarakatsani

30

I'LL ALWAYS BE THERE

Sunlight filters through the trees
Slips pasts the window
To reach his pillow
But he's not there
He is long gone
With the laughters and moans
Leaving me with the silence,
It was deafening at first,
Shattering all my trust,
Soughting help in lust,
In the end, I just,
Gave up and did what was must,
I washed my tear stained face,
They can't stay at my place,
But who's worthy enough to fill this space,
I looked up and saw someone familiar,
There's a girl standing in the mirror,
her hairs dishevelled like she came out of a storm,
She was maybe in the state of mourn,
But she has a soul and her own place to call home,
And I think she can sew back my torned pieces,
I think I'm ready to take this journey from you to me,

To be free from your haunting memories,
The sunlight filters through the trees,
And slips pasts the window,
Reaching for my pillow,
Playing with my hair,
Because no matter what,
I'll always be there.

by Grace Heart

31

IN RETROSPECT

In retrospect, those days were the hardest,
Sleepless nights and the damp pillow was a secret,
My pain wasn't as I couldn't fake a smile.
All alone... desperate and frightened.
The world was talking but I heard nothing,
Time stopped bothering me... a day felt like a decade,
Even the music and nature which was once my favourite
stood as strangers,
Screamed out of anger... cried out of frustration,
Waited for my death to embrace me,
Thought that my wounds and scars would follow me to my
grave,
At some point I felt the need to wake up for the people who
love me,
Started giving them what they want... My time, my ears,
love, care...
I was dead inside.
The happiness I gave others started to reflect on me... It
gave me life.
It nurtured me from an egg to a butterfly,
They sucked out my pain,
Healed my wounds with the magic of selfless love,

Now I have risen from the dead.
Survived something that demanded my life,
Moving forward with utmost gratitude.

by Amala Susan Roy

32

LET'S ACKNOWLEDGE ANXIETY

The excessive worry wouldn't pause,
Everything seems like a huge loss.
Past, present & future
All yet none can be a trigger.
For someone feeling very anxious,
Coping strategies can become a huge fuss,
'Don't worry, everything will be okay!'
May not be helpful words to say.
Yoga, meditation and deep breathing may be favourable,
But sometimes the person may still feel disabled.
Seeking help from a mental health professional,
Can help you understand your anxiety better.
Feeling anxious is natural,
Asking for help should be normal.
Anxiety is a feeling that you may face,
Let's learn to cope and control it with grace!

by Anushka Kharbanda

33

WHEN A PSYCHOLOGIST CAME TO RESCUE

The queer noise in her mind,
Forced her to stay behind.
The broken heart and sad soul,
Didn't want to live anymore.
The past was gloomy she knew,
She tried diverting the mind through paint, dance and sew,
But nothing brought her the inner peace,
She tried until she got down to her knees.
One fine day a man came,
A psychologist who was well known to fame.
He empathized with her as no one did,
Tried to help her bit by bit.
Three to four sessions in a week,
Helped her to achieve and seek,
Every bit of that mental peace,
That once she lost now tried to seize.
And now after a year we know her
As someone whose laughs are funnier,
That the joke she herself made,
A stand-up comedian can never fade.

by Anushka Kharbanda

34

ONE OF THOSE NIGHTS

The ride home was strangely quiet
The radio sounds separate
however, my mind was deafening
like a thunderstorm on October evening

The house was vacant
Yet the spirits of my memories
exist in my head for centuries
Never knowing when to leave

But then day turns to a moonless night
The chilly air accompanied by the faint light
As my mind shifts into an unexplainable sadness

Questioning myself thousands of unnecessary things to fret
All the things I wish I could say
All the negative things I could think of,
How I'm not good enough, and never will
I tell myself that nobody cares
And my brain keeps replaying
dumb things that troubled me
I feel like a fool, yet still

I don't know what to do
But time will still go by
The night will meet the dawn as before
And just another day, we'll rise once more
Leaving all of our demons aside
And continue finding things to stay alive for.

by Sellina Mutiara

35

HELP ME

All it takes is just a slight trigger
And everything is falling apart again
This constant battle in my mind
It's a war that I never win
Once I almost did
But almost is never enough.

I tried so hard
Yet it seems like it's not enough
still not enough.
Hell, what does enough even mean
I don't know anymore
High expectations,
and shattered reality.

Hold me tight tonight
Keep me company
At least until the sunrise
Cause I've got a monster inside my head
It won't shut up
Moreover, it wants me dead.

Stay, and help me go through this
Thus, we can fly together instead.

by Sellina Mutiara

36

POSITIONS

Waking up with an unconscious state of soul,
Over thinking about the dolour.
Regretting every moment in despair,
Calling out the wounds to expire!

The talk of the moments we hark,
Nostalgic memories aren't always dark.
I convince myself that everything will be alright;
I just have to be swift with my hands tight!

Alone mentally - a wont friend of mine,
From morning till the dine.
I kept myself aloof from them,
Felt like futile in the realm.

Yet I conceived the strength within me,
Not counting the difficulty.
Crying to sleep with no motive,
But I always tried to be innovative.

Regretting the times I misdirected,
But I'll forgive the mistakes I created.
No matter how much I remorse my feelings,
I am a human at all the endings.

I defined self-love as loving myself,
With right decisions, paths and self-help.
Without hurting anyone and not being selfish,
Because conclusively, mental peace is the fetish.

I'm extremely strong but my heart is delicate,
I collect my aesthetics to rise and educate.
Being kind is heavenly not a weakness,
Vulnerability is my strength and positivity is my happiness.

I've been experiencing different positions in my life,
Blessing you to enchant your state of mind!

by Suchitra Satapathy

37

SAYONARA

You never know,
When it's
Going to be
Your last time;
To catch up with
An old friend;
To witness their
Entrancing grin;
Or to stand under the
Same sky as they;
For you believe,
There shall be more;
You think you might
Have an eternity; until
You snap out of
The mere fantasy
And discern
You do not
And it's too late;
So you're left behind; to
Cherish the beautiful memories

You have of them
And pray with all you have
To The Lord
That He may
Grant their soul
Eternal peace
As they journey to
The other part
Of this world.

by Rida Hassan

38

SELF-LOVE

I found it in the end,
the song in my heartbeat,
joy running through my veins,
peace within my being,
the love I searched for.
For so long,
buried within,
masked by doubt,
sitting in the darkness,
waiting to be discovered,
to be set free.
That love,
the love I craved for,
I've claimed,
for myself,
and self alone.

by Samantha Marsters

39

SELF-ACCEPTANCE

I wish to paint my body,
with the colours I lack,
I point out each one of my flaws,
and side-line my every perfection,
as if I'm always searching,
for a reason to degrade myself.
I'm all in when it comes to lecture
about self-love,
but seldom do I practice it.
I can go on and on,
writing about self-acceptance,
only for it to be trapped forever,
amongst my ceaseless self-loathing.
I never thought that one day,
living in my own body,
would feel like a task to me.
How can I ever expect to top your priority list,
when I always come last on mine?

by Nitya Aggarwal

40

THE GOLD WITHIN

searching for love all around,
heartbroken I trod,
cursing and blaming myself,
unbeknownst of self-love
till the gold within shimmered,
seeping through my unhealed cracks,
revealing my inner self,
and transforming all the hate
into the love I sought.

by Nitya Aggarwal

41

SHAME ON THEM

There is no shame in admitting you're not at your best,
That you spend your nights crying and your days lying in
bed,
That it is not laziness or lack of interest which keeps you
there,
But the strongest feeling of helplessness you've ever felt.
Life didn't come with instructions, you heartily protest,
Your voice barely above a whisper in fear of their
judgement.
You know the sting of their words better than most,
It's what keeps you saying you are fine when you are not.
If you speak up they will think you are crazy or worse,
They will make you believe you are completely alone.
Shame on them for tricking you to think so,
Because you know what? You are none of those.

You're no less for needing help when life catches up to your
mind,
Or when you feel that you can't do anything right.
You must know that the hopelessness you feel won't simply
vanish,
You will need time and assistance to overcome it.

If life is a stream that branches and branches,
It is bound to sometimes encounter obstacles.
But like the river takes turns to surpass them,
You must persist and not yield to this hurdle.
If you speak up they will think you are a burden,
They will make you believe you were bound to feel like this.
Shame on them that can't tell weakness from strength,
Because you know what? Strength is what it takes to ask for help.

No one can blame you if suddenly things don't seem real,
If you're feeling so much at the same time that you can't deal.
They will tell you it is only sadness, and maybe it will make you angry,
Ridding your mind from the emptiness that so easily sat there.
It's alright, we've all felt like that at some point, and whoever says not,
Are deluding themselves so badly it's not even a lie anymore.
It's alright, if figuring out what you feel takes longer than they expect,
Or if your mind mutes it all so you are not overwhelmed.
If you speak up they will say stress and pressure got to you,
They will make you believe it is a shortcoming of yours.
Shame on them who say you'll never be good enough,
Because you know what? In this, too, they are wrong.

by Eider Muñiz Mercadal

42

THE WELL

You're inside an old well,
hidden so deeply in the earth's entrails,
alone and without the means to get out
and it's raining, making the water's level rise.

You're inside an old well,
and it's not your fault you're there,
when others pushed you without warning
over its low edge.

It's raining and the water's level is rising,
it reaches past your calves,
when the hunger starts to cry out
to your pained insides.

The water doesn't stop, it keeps going up,
until your chest is swallowed by its cold grasp
and the thirst that it can't quench
has cruelly gripped your heart.

The water's past your neck and you still don't realise
that loneliness is sometimes worse than any pain,
but you have something none can take,
a soul and voice to call out for help.

It is not the fear of drowning that makes your heart beat
faster and faster as you hear footsteps near,
but nonetheless it makes your eyes lift up to the sky
and see a hole so far that you'd forgotten about.

Your eyes feel like they're burning,
but you won't look away;
you force yourself to stare, because:
Is that the sun up there?

Your eyes must really be burning,
just like your breath's frozen in your chest,
by the time a small shadow
covers you in its shade.

You want to protest and feel that sweet pain again,
until a voice reaches your ears: is someone there?
Your reticence vanishes as fast as it appeared
and your own voice echoes over the stone's surface.

You can't see her face
nor the surprise you're sure must be there
as she looks down at you
deep in the well, with the water around your neck.

Contrary to what most would expect,
you warn her away and, in the process,
reveal all the pain and loneliness
that's been festering in your chest.

She's stubborn, though,
and does not move
and you can't tell why she stays
next to your ugly well.

Unknown to you she's wandered the fields,
where flowers grow and birds sing,
and gone unnoticed amongst all
under the sun's fair glow.

She has known a different hunger,
her heart a different thirst,
pain wasn't a constant companion,
but her soul's yearning was the same.

It's the first well she encounters
and she still hasn't learnt
to fear that endless darkness
that all at one point face.

She's too close to the edge,
which makes you shout at her,
but she ignores your fearful rage
and dangles her feet over the abyss.

She throws you a rope
and you look at it
as if your eyes can't decipher
what its purpose is.

If she'd given you a snake,
you might have looked more kindly at her,
but she's not deterred even when
you try again to frighten her away.

She listens without judgement,
not moving up there,
braving the sun, the rain
and all kinds of weather.

But she's a creature of light
and hasn't learnt to fear the darkness
and doubt gnaws your insides
the way for hope alighting.

The rope's still dangling
and you wonder what she'd say,
if she knew that every night
you climbed it to watch her as she slept.

One day you forget to return to your well,
and she's awake before you realise,
and watches you with those big eyes
for the first time under the light.

Her hands reach out,
wonder written over her face,
and you almost flinch away
when you notice her trembling.

Her lack of fear and trust
leave such a deep mark,
that you soon realise
you need not go back.

There will be no more hunger,
there will be no more thirst,
for she'll brave your deep well
and you'll face her empty fields.

by Eider Muñiz Mercadal

43

STRESS

Stress is a double-edged sword:
It can hurt you and those you hold close.
But it's so hard to avoid its hold,
When today's world refuses to slow.
How are you supposed to not be tense,
When there are deadlines everywhere?
When people around you all rush through life,
With no care for overloading their minds?
You think the problem is all yours,
And keep pushing despite the warning signs.
You don't realise how that can burn you out,
Or that you may not be the only one,
That will have to pay the price.
Instead, take a moment to think; slow down.
Look around, you're not the only one.
Those closest to you worry you're not fine.
'Cause you're not fine, but that's alright:
Everyone needs help once in a while.
Forget the strain and simply breathe,
Block out everything else,
Until the bustle from outside fades,
Until you can hear your mind again.

You can be fine and help those you love,
If you just take some time to unwind.
And what if that fails to be enough?
Well, seeking aid has never been a crime.

by Eider Muñiz Mercadal

44

SPEAK, IT WILL BE OKAY

"I don't know how sure you can be in your state of mind
about your decisions
but isn't mental health supposed to be talked about
and not suppressed?

Isn't it supposed to be let out in the open,
to be talked about
rather than be hidden behind our faux smiles?

Your anxieties and worries are a part of you,
even though you may not like them.
And you have to brave yourself for every challenge
that comes your way because that is how you live.

If you get miserable in life, please don't give up
because it's just a tough tide,
and it will pass.

But if you get really tired and exhausted of breathing in
misery,
It's okay to stop and think.
It's okay if you want to let go.

Sometimes you can't bear everything...
Our capacity is limited and sometimes,
our life gives us so much misery, it exceeds our limits.

So, it's okay.
Don't beat yourself up for things you couldn't get over
because
Hurt isn't supposed to be gotten over,
it is supposed to be allowed to heal properly with care.

But if you feel like you're suffocating and
you need to speak, speak.
Speak your throat sore.
Shout it out to the world.
Don't be afraid of them for judging you,
because you know that they will.
It's human nature, sometimes it can't be helped.

But you, you are valiant, my love.
And you will soar so high in the sky that looks
so dark to you now because it is lightning and thundering
but
once this storm passes, you'll fly like a
bird out of its cage for the first time in its life."

by Sudipti Saha

45

STRUGGLING AND HEALING

Been having palpitations, been feeling stressed.
Moods have been changing, and I can't concentrate.
Tired all the time, but I can't sleep.
They said I've been hallucinating.
They said I've been delusional.
My appetite has changed, barely or excessively eating.
Drugs have been on my mind,
distracting me from suicidal thoughts.
Something is wrong with me, but what exactly?
Anxiety, depression, anorexia, bulimia, psychotic disorders
and more,
Whichever one is it?
I don't know.
Do I need to be fixed?
I don't know either.
All I know is that,
my mental health is getting bad again,
and I'm determined to get better.
I'm drowning,
but I can swim.
I'm struggling,
But I'm healing.

I'm not losing hope yet.

I know I'll get better.
To those who are struggling right now,
please hold on.
You are strong enough to get through this.
You may be struggling right now,
but you're healing.
I have faith in you.
Now, you have to believe in yourself too.

by Adela Lily

46

SUICIDAL JOURNEY

My heart is in pieces,
as sharp as they fall,
Perfect to end it all.
I look down into
the reflection,
As I see a face,
So tired and soaked,
As she bleeds red tears,
From her internal fears,
Yet I feel as though I know
Her name..
She is ruined poor thing,
and oh so cold,
such an empty soul...
With silence in her eyes,
that screams her hidden cry's,
from many closed ears,
she's been fighting for years,
And Suddenly,
I remember her name....
She is me,
A Lost soul who longs

to be free...

A journey that needed saving
with a life worth craving...
All I needed was a hero,
and that superwoman
was me,
and the broken pieces are now
my masterpiece.

by Brianna Kidd

47

THE OCEAN

Someday,
I would run to the beach,
Feel myself against the breeze,
Let my feet sink in.

These vast ocean in front of me,
Sometimes I wonder, if utopia exist,
I only see raging waves,
Constantly battling so that they reach.

But one voice tells me,
''Believe, there is paradise that everyone misses.''

by Adlina Khusairi

48

THINGS WILL GET BETTER

There are lot of things,
Going in your mind,
Your thoughts are exploding,
And are unbind.

I can see the pain,
In your eyes,
There's a darkness in you,
Where your thought lies.

The world will judge you,
But don't you give up.

I can understand,
There's going a lot,
But first you've to
Let go of all those thoughts.

I know, it's easy to say.
But trust me honey,
Things will get nice,
Once again the sun will
Conquer your thoughts, & rise.

by Nehali Naik

49

TOMORROW WILL BE BETTER

Feels so numb, yet so alive.
I cloak my blemished wrists, I descend.
Not seeking love, nor an end.
Soaking the warm blood, drying cascading tears.
Yearning for pain, stroking scars in reminiscence.
Oh love! What do I do to revive?

Prisoner of one's thoughts, no place to hide.
I hear my brain scream, I sink deep below.
Not seeking light, nor a shallow end.
Giving into dear darkness, putting on a facade.
Shattering my graceful ruins, nothing left ahead.
Oh love! It's high time I revive.

A place which ruined you, cannot heal you.
I move ahead, in search of lost smiles.
The sun shines a little brighter here, woods paving path.
Mountains coalesce to laugh at your futile worries.
Stars twinkle applauding the moon, yet again it has come.

And so will I, I tell myself,
Tomorrow shall be better!
I toil every day, to see if it arrived.

by Preethi

ACKNOWLEDGMENTS

I'd like to start off by saying I am most grateful to my parents, as without them I wouldn't be where I am today. They've never doubted me once and have always agreed to stand where I did.

Secondly, I'd like to thank my friends, especially Tia (who is also a co-author of this book). Thank you for being there when I needed it the most.

a special acknowledgement to my readers, who have kept me going through my hardest times, thank you so much.

Last, but not the least, I'd also like to take the time to thank all the co-authors of this book and Inkfeathers for being so patient and hard-working with me on this.

MEET THE CO-AUTHORS

Laure Lacornette

Laure Lacornette (@laulacospoetry) is a France-born author. Her words are deep, and she has a very unique way of expressing herself through words. She hopes that the people who read her words will find some kind of resonance and/or healing.

Maria Wynnckyj

Maria Wynnyckyj works at a state university and she enjoys writing in her spare time. She is a proud mother of three grown children and currently 2 grandchildren. You can connect with her on Instagram @mariawyn316.

Archana Natarajan

Archana is a Bengaluru based blogger who likes to write in the romantic fiction and travelogue genres. Her stories have been published in over ten anthologies. She has also authored scientific articles as a Biochemist and is pursuing her Ph.D in Neurochemistry. Apart from blogging at http://aworldofcolors.blogspot.com, she also dabbles in candid wedding photography with her husband. Currently, she is utilizing her creative juices in compiling interesting stories that she can share with her son as he is growing up. You can connect with on Instagram @archanavaidyanathan.

A Low Kick

Lakshya Nitin Tandon a.k.a A-Low-Kick is an aspiring poet and writer. A-Low-Kick, his pen-name, when read out together comes out as the Hindi word 'अलौकिक' which translates to 'Supernatural' in English, by which he means to tell the world that his work is as 'supernatural' as his pen-name. He is from India and currently studies in IIT Jodhpur.

Valerie Hernandez

Originally from Mexico, Valerie Hernandez is an economist and a digital strategist for NGOs with a master's degree in communication and digital media, but a writer for love. However, she loves music, literature, traveling, taking pictures, and telling stories so much that she also collaborates independently with various print and digital publications, where she writes about pop culture, music, and concerts. She also tours and manages social media for artists, musicians, and bands. Her first novel "FRENTE AL ESCENARIO", is available now in all digital bookstores.

Dhwanie Shetty

Dhwanie Shetty is a 16-year-old writer and poet. For her, writing is a way of expressing herself without any limits and conditions. This is her second published work in an anthology, and she wishes to publish her own book in the future. You can find more of her work on Instagram @thelastpagesofmynotebook

Mara Martins

Mara, currently studying in educational sciences, has many passions, one of them being writing in English and French, sometimes she also likes to express herself in German or Portuguese. Thoughts, short stories, but mostly poetry. As a sensitive person, she aspires to fill her words with emotions, to let the readers feel something, being it sadness and emptiness or joy and ardour. A dream of hers is to publish a book of her own.

Aishwarya Shukla

Aishwarya is a 16-year-old writer, and she has been writing for the last 5 years. She writes to communicate with others, to stimulate interest or action from the reader. She has an Instagram handle where she constantly keeps posting her writings - @scent.of.my.thoughts She uses writing to help her reflect on her own experiences as well as putting her views on a greater platform . Her hobbies include reading, anchoring, and writing -which play a main role for her having vocational views. Her writing helps you to see the parts of life that are euphoric and intriguing.

Nehal Gandhi

Nehal is a 13-year-old living in Sweden, who loves reading and writing and creating ANYTHING! From essays for an assignment, to pages and pages of creativity and imagination, she likes it all. She wants to publish a novel someday, and this is her very first published work, but she hopes for more soon.

Yohan Acosta

Yohan is an English language and literature teacher as well as a volunteer ambassador of Enrich HK, an NGO in Hong Kong that empowers migrant workers to their financial literacy and education. A creative writer at heart, Yohan  writes poetry and prose with humanistic and philosophical themes. She is a blogger as well who runs www.psychcatalog.com, a website that aims to promote mental health and personal development. She can be reached on Instagram at @_yohanacosta_, Facebook @AcostaYohan and Pinterest @_yohanacosta_.

Athena Thiyam

Athena Thiyam is a 19-year-old poet hailing from Imphal, Manipur. She is currently pursuing a BA degree in English, Psychology and Sociology, along with honours in English Literature at MCM DAV College for Women, Chandigarh. She has published her first book of poems titled 'The Other World and others' when she turned 13 and is currently working on her next one. She loves to read a lot and spends her spare time with her three cats. She can be reached on her Instagram at: @_ergane_

Ishwari Salunke

Ishwari is a 17-year-old student from Mumbai. She likes to read and listen to music in her free time. She is a classical music enthusiast. She likes composing poems and essays and hopes to make an impact by her writings someday.

Malay Mundra

Malay draws his inspiration for writing by observing the vast chasm of random things that he sees on the internet and the physical world. He thinks of writing as an art form that helps him articulate his own thoughts, watch him try triumphing over a journey of self-discovery on Instagram @malay_tries.

Rebecca Hilliard

Rebecca Hilliard is an author and a mental health advocate. She is the author of Heaven's Heartbeat and A World Locked Away. She is passionate about helping those with mental illness know they aren't alone. She's currently focusing on her own trauma work as well as her mental health Instagram account @inthistogethernow_. In her free time, she likes to kayak, bike, write, and snuggle with her dog Bella.

Keegan Cockin

Keegan is a 19-year-old writer hailing from South Africa, who loves playing instruments (especially guitar and drums), and spending time with his pets and painting. He writes songs and poems and hopes to publish his own songs and poems in the future.

His Instagram handle is @keeganzachariah

Vidhi Jain

Vidhi is a 17-year-old budding writer residing in India Who hopes to create a difference in the writing community and has colossal fondness for poetry. She loves travelling, reading books, and learning new things. An innovative writer with new skills, Vidhi writes poetry about pain, escapism, and humanistic themes. Follow her on Instagram @vidhispoems.

Despina Sarakatsani

Despina is a digital creator, and a university student from Greece, majoring in Environmental Science. Writing is a hobby and a form of self-expression for her. When she's not writing, she enjoys travelling, listening to good music, and being  close to nature. She aspires to one day be able to create content that inspires people and makes a difference in the world. She can be reached on Instagram @cherrybaddie.

Grace Heart

 Grace Heart is a girl in her early twenties who always felt alienated, but there's one place where she feels accepted and that's in between her words. She is a flower that has learnt to bloom in the darkness of this world and appreciate its beauty in every way possible. You can take a stroll in the streets of her mind through her Instagram @elle___aye and look at the skies from her eyes. P.S - Black coffee with 2 scoops of anxiety is her favourite drink.

Eider Muñiz Mercadal

Eider is a 23-year-old Spanish who loves to write and read, but let's not forget their passion for animals, painting and learning new things. Those are the things that drive them forward every day and now, hopefully, these poems will be the first push needed for other people to keep pressing forward too.

Amala Susan Roy

Amala is a 23-year-old girl from India and she is an engineer by profession. She is more good with writing down thoughts in a diary rather than expressing them. Only later those thoughts evolved to poems and now poems help her connect to people.

She loves to read books, to dance, to travel and adventures. She can be reached on Instagram @canopytales.

Sellina Mutiara

Sellina is a 17-year-old student from Indonesia who received academic scholarship 2 years in a row in school. Writing, singing, and playing the piano is her passion. Her goal is to touch many people's hearts and bring awareness about mental health issues through her poetry. She hopes that this book could help and educate people about mental health better. She can be reached on Instagram @celestinewords & @ssellinnaa.

Anushka Kharbanda

Anushka is a passionate learner with over 21 years of experience in life skills such as empathy, resilience, creative thinking, and interpersonal relationship skills! For reading about Anushka's views on life visit

insighttolight.wordpress.com & @Insight_to_light on Instagram.

Suchitra Satapathy

Suchitra is a kind & a sweetheart human. She is an engineering student and she has her brains into different programming languages. She is a speaker as well as a social activist. She loves to support everyone. She is an editor & creator, running pages on Instagram @exhaling_words & @thesuchitra. She wants her life as an aesthetic ray of sun, and she is ready to conquer all the hurdles and troubles with grace.

Rida Hassan

Rida Hassan is the Islamabad (Kamra) based author of Sayonara. Enamoured by the literary as a young girl, she has scribbled extempore poetry on digital platforms for many years. Her poems have also been featured in the magazine SMASH. Her latest piece bears a distinct mark of her experiences as a medical student. Rida is usually found either chasing sunsets amidst her strolls or absorbed in yet another mystery novel. You can connect with her on Instagram @risorusprocurus.

Samantha Marsters

Samantha is a 36-year-old from New Zealand who uses the pen name 'ShesJustSammy'. Samantha is an amateur poetry writer, writing of life, its lessons and what she has learnt and the person she's becoming. You can connect with her on Instagram @shesjustsammy.

Nitya Aggarwal

Nitya is a 17-year-old ambivert from Delhi who finds solace in poetry. She wrote her first poem in 2015 and that was when she realised that she had a thing for literature and poetry inside her. Writing brings her the ultimate joy and she thinks of as a therapy

which can express the loudest thoughts silently. You can connect with her on Instagram @glimpseofmywords.

Sudipti Saha

Sudipti Saha is born and brought up in Nagpur, Maharashtra. She is the author of 'Life, Love, Heartbreak & A Taste of Freedom', which is available on Amazon. She is passionate about writing as well as loves a good fantasy story any time of the day and has a deep appreciation for books. She can be reached through Instagram @t.belletrist or Email at sudiptisaha@gmail.com

Adela Lily

This is Adela, a 16-year-old aspiring writer from Hong Kong. Writing is therapy for her and she hopes that her words can bring hope to readers who are going through a hard time, and let them know they're not alone. If you wish to connect with her, do visit @adelalk_ or @poetryalk on Instagram!

Brianna Kidd

Brianna is a 25-year-old free-spirited individual, who has a strong passion for capturing the depths of emotions and transpiring them into poetry. She has always been someone who finds beauty in emotions especially the ability to feel others even in silence. Also, Brianna has dreams to become a writer, where she will publish a collection of poetry books living out her dreams and passions. You can connect with her on Instagram @poetofdepth.

Preethi

Preethi is a 23-year-old from Hyderabad, India. She loves to travel, to meet new people and to find herself within. She loves poetry which makes you contemplate and aspires you to write more of that kind.

Adlina Khusairi

Adlina Khusairi, is a lyrics enthusiast and medical graduate of UiTM Malaysia. With being endless passionate about BTS songs and lyrics, she makes her poetry debut as a co-author of Untangled. Adlina has been a lifelong writer and first began creating worlds and characters through her writing from the age of 14. She lives and works out of her home in the suburbs of Kuala Lumpur and loves spending her weekends listening to BTS's discography while studying. To connect with Adlina on Instagram, visit @poetry.bts.

Nehali Naik

Nehali Naik is a 20-year-old aspiring writer and artist from Mumbai, who discovered her interest in writing and painting during this pandemic. Apart from reading & writing she loves listening to music. She believes, "When you're afraid to say your thoughts out loud you write it down and gift wrap it in the form of poetry". She loves fiction because it's an escape from reality. In addition, Nehali is an Accounting & Finance student who wants to become a published author & recognized artist someday. You can connect with her on Instagram at @themusingtales and @_nehalii_.

INKFEATHERS PUBLISHING

India's Most Author Friendly Publishing House

Stay updated about latest books, anthologies, events,
exclusive offers, contests, product giveaways and other things
that we do to support authors.

f   Inkfeathers Publishing

◎   @InkfeathersPublishing

𝕏   @_Inkfeathers

in   @Inkfeathers

⊕   Inkfeathers.com

We'd love to connect with you!

Made in the USA
Middletown, DE
09 July 2021